building

a

village

volume three

pamela fields

S.H.E. PUBLISHING, LLC

Building A Village | Volume Three
Copyright © 2021 by Pamela Fields.

All rights reserved. Printed in the United States of America. No part of this book may be used or reproduced in any manner whatsoever without written permission except in the case of brief quotations embodied in critical articles or reviews.

For information contact :
info@shepublishingllc.com
www.shepublishingllc.com

Book Cover and Title Page design by Michelle Phillips of
CHELLD3 3D VISUALIZATION AND DESIGN

ISBN :
9781953163356 (paperback)

First Edition : December 2021

10 9 8 7 6 5 4 3 2 1

CONTENTS

1 | TO MY SONS:

2 | PURPOSE OF STRUGGLE

3 | THE WORD OF TRUTH

4 | TURN THE CURSE INTO A BLESSING

5 | THE HARDEST GIFT TO GIVE

6 | OPPORTUNITIES TO GIVE

7 | A NEW FOCUS

8 | A SPIRIT OF MIDNIGHT

9 | AN INTRODUCTION TO SELF

10 | A REACH BEYOND MY GRIP

11 | THE ROAD TO FREEDOM'S DOOR

12 | ONCE WHITE, WHITE NO MORE

13 | I CRIED, I PRAYED, I FOUGHT

14 | BARRIERS

15 | A GOOD STEWARD

16 | LIFEGUARD

17 | BRINGING DELIVERANCE NTO FOCUS

18 | WINTER IS

19 | LEARNING TO FIGHT THE DEVIL

20 | GIVING AWAY A MIRACLE

21 | HELP! LOVED ONE FOR RANDSOM

22 | THE BEST TEACHER

23 | OUR OWN CHILDREN ARE AT STAKE

24 | GIFTS THAT LAST

25 | ALL OF OUR CHILDREN ARE STARS

INTERMISSION

26 | THE FACE OF CRIME

27 | SOLUTIONS

28 | OUR CHILD NEED

29 | COME AS MY GUEST

30 | NO OUTLET

31 | WHOSE CHOICE

32 | A POCKET FULL OF JOY

33 | WITH ALL THE THINGS I KNOW TO DO

34 | FAITH REMOVES THE CHALLENGE

35 | A SKETCH OF BEAUTY

36 | CUTTING ON THE LIGHT IN DARKNESS

37 | PORTRIAT OF A SERVANT

38	MORE THAN YOU CAN IMAGINE
39	THIS OLD WORLD HAS A HEAVEN
40	A GARDEN OF FLOWERS
41	OLE MY RAGGEDY SOUL
42	A SHADOW IN THE HEART
43	FREEDOM MEANS CHOICES
44	THE PRAYER OF A SERVANT
45	THE VOICE OF GOD
46	SHALLOW WAVES
47	LIVING THROUGH THE STORM
48	THE WORD NEXT
49	A COLOR SPLASH
50	FIRST LIGHT A.D.
	ACKNOWLEDGMENTS
	ABOUT THE AUTHOR

building

a

village

volume three

pamela fields

1 | TO MY SONS:

This is to my sons,
        And believe me
           I have many.

As my responsibility,
        I've acquired in this land
           Is to provide a place of refuge.

Working with
        My daughters
           Wherever possible

But my sons,
        These words
           I share.

Your world is too tiny
        And the universe is big enough
           For you to stay hidden in it.

You travel around in this tight space
        So cramped because a large part of it
           Is the dark corners of your own mind.

A world of information
        Travels around you, going places
           And making it, many do by comparison.

PAMELA FIELDS

Yet you've enclosed yourself in a tight fit
    A corner and you can't back your way out
        Can't climb out and can't dig yourself out

Only one way out and
    The one thing before you is
        The things which you allow

A negative audience in which
    To host tis all you can investigate
        Because you won't explore others

Many have said
    That Columbus
        Never discovered America…

But you must agree that the man
    Had to know that there was another
        World outside of his own.

You hold the keys to
    Your own dark dungeon
        Your cruel mentality won't even set you free.

Aw. Come on, let yourself out!
    Put yourself in some new
        Situations every day!

Live a little!
    Feed and
        Nourish your mind!

The torment that you put
    Yourself through is worst
        Than that of any slave master.

BUILDING A VILLAGE

My point is this…
    What do you know besides:
        The classroom
        The home front
        Someone else's house
        Your girl
        And maybe jail
        The hospital
        And the police station?

There is a war on the street
    The fight may seem physical
        But really it's not…

It's a bunch of others,
    Your brothers who
        Are trapped just like you.

Finding the torment too
    Much to take as the walls
        Close in on them like a sweat box.

Responsibilities that slip through
    Your fingers, and that's when
        The real pressure comes.

I will not die
    Without
        Making you aware…

That your challenge is not physical
    It's not with your brothers
    It's not with your parents
    Or other authoritative figures
    It's really is not even in the classroom
        Although you can find the answers you seek
        A slow process

PAMELA FIELDS

      But that's because you're ready for something
      And you're ready for it now!

Your challenge my son
    Is within, the way out
        Is inside of you.

But because you limit your resources
    Because you have not sought out other parts of this world
        You're stuck in a status-quo

Many have
    Stereo typed
        You because of it.

You're holding on to a brown paper bag,
    Only big enough to fit a can of pop
        But you won't let go

Where there is
    An endless supply
        Of shopping bags at your disposal

Your worth and your wealth
    Fit the size of the bag
        You're holding on to

Like tiny squirrel
    Its greatest reward is
        The treasure it finds inside the shell of a nut.

2 | PURPOSE OF STRUGGLE

I struggle through life
    On purpose.

That purpose grips my survival
    And takes me where I want to go

Right back to a struggle of the fragile soul
    Of a people, precious and destitute for time

A want, a need, a hunger
    Against a ticking end

Where time is not an ally
    And my purpose is still a struggle.

3 | THE WORD OF TRUTH

The gospel of Jesus Christ
    Is written where the passages
        And quotes of the words of
            Jesus are printed in red.

Like the tin foil
    Which wraps the freshness
        Of a stick of Wrigley's gum

So are various other passages
    Of the written truth as it is
        Recorded in the Bible
            Wrapped in foils of gold.

Releasing a fresh revelation
    For instruction that's so intricate
        Its importance leading you to
            Another step in higher living

A step which helps you to
    Become deaf, totally illiterate
        And dying to the ways of the flesh
            Which causes destruction and bondage

A golden foil which unravels
    The revelation truth, and
        When applied to your life
            Places direction in proper perspective.

4 | TURN THE CURSE INTO A BLESSING

Like the ugly duckling
   Turned into a beautiful swan...

So too must all of us be when the enemy
   Has seemed to have taken over.

5 | THE HARDEST GIFT TO GIVE

The hardest gift to give
    Is the gift that purges
        The inner man's soul

The gift that helps a
    Man, woman, boy or girl
        To be well in their spirit.

Like the truth when
    It hurts, because it hurts
        Is it any less the truth?

Medicine, bitter and
    Tastes bad. But it's the
        Same medicine which makes well.

There are some gifts,
    The gift of discipline
    And the gift of obedience
    The gift of humility
    Longsuffering and even
    Faith in a way…

When all things appear
    To be at its worse, faith being
        The only witness that it's not.

Being chastised with
    The rod of correction. Words which
        Places all of us in the path of righteous growth.

BUILDING A VILLAGE

Every labor of love, makes it no
    Less painful, but rather a work and a joy together
        With the anticipated outcome of spreading good tidings

Gifts of birth comes with
    Labors of love. God gave His only
        Begotten Son, because He loved man.

Jesus gave His life in much
    Humility, pain and suffering.
        An act of love in an effort to redeem man.

But a gift is given, it's an
    Opportunity to share of oneself.
        Anything else is merely an exchange of presents.

It's not just the gift, but
    The giver. And the transaction is not
        Complete unless the receiver accepts in the same fate.

6 | OPPORTUNITIES TO GIVE

With his last breath
He wouldn't let the
Coins go.

The opportunity came once
When his only sister was stricken with cancer
But he wouldn't give anything to help her.

Holding on with all his might
Nothing to profit by merely looking
At these worldly treasures

Another opportunity came one snowy
Christmas Eve's night, when all was not well
Cause this mother's children were cold and hungry

But still this man looked the other way
Saying that she was a bad mother, judging her
Because she stole and used drugs.

And so he let them suffer
Instead of listening to the
Soft, kind voice of his conscience

And hardened his heart instead of listening
To the voice which said, "when you give to another, you
Allow what you have to grow in your hands and in the life of others."

BUILDING A VILLAGE

Still another opportunity came the time
When his wife was very ill and he saw
Nothing but a liability.

All her fruitful years, she blessed him
Tried to be a good wife through it all and no one
Would have ever known how much she laboured with this marriage

So when the lonely old man
Gave up the ghost, he should have known that
Naked he came into the world, and naked would he return

And so the coins were found clenched in his fists,
He wouldn't let them go, and only death
Could separate him and his riches.

7 | A NEW FOCUS

In my less than perfect world
I allowed my focus to fall
On aches and pains
Misfortunes and mishaps

Everything can be wrong if you let it.

But in these times when
Things are so less than perfect
This is the time to let go
And to turn your focus around.

To realize a greater principle
Rules life's mishaps
And begin to focus on
Things that bring good cheer.

8 | A SPIRIT OF MIDNIGHT

My path takes me right through
    Midnight ally, an obstacle of much dread.

Freight that goes boo in the dark
    An all kinds of terrors

Screeching winds
    Cut throats and robbers

Owls that go hoot-hoot
    And all sorts of creeping things

Spider webs and
    Wicked dreams, nightmares, and ghost

Hair raising thrills
    Twilight hour, against a gloomy dark blue moonlit sky

The spirit of midnight places
    You right there

Cat cries
    And dogs' howl

Once again
    The freaks come out

Many ills pay a night call
    And many sleep and don't wake up

PAMELA FIELDS

Sprit of thunder clashes
      And its companion lightening

Midnight horror calls
      And they all come out the closet

Undercover crimes
      And street walking troubles

Come dealing
      At the all-night markets

Gunsmoke and rough play
      Mysterious bodies left to discover

A real live jungle
      Of choices, triggers and dares, oh my

Getting through to the other side
      Is a spirit stirring up in my soul

Cause somehow, I must break through
      This barrier to a brand-new day

Where hope brightly shines like
      The rays of the sun's glow

And the midnight's terror is far behind
      Suffocated in the memory and cease to remain

Pardon me for my shrewd force of intentions
      But I must wake on the other side of this fearsome midnight

Skeletons with bucked eyes
      Sounds in the night that speak

Sleepless hours
      Tossing and turning

Deep sleep fits
      Of chills and night sweats

BUILDING A VILLAGE

Troublesome times are coming near the end
    Of its road, day break soon to come after while

Long overdue, this two-timing sin
    Causing me to suffer twice

Once, in a court of law, doors slam
    And keys rattle, locking away the sun's glow

Twice, within my own heart, my spirit
    Suffers in the dungeon of moaning and regret

Cold and numb
    From the pain of the night

Now I see that I'm the
    One who closed the doors

Afraid to go through the midnight
    And face those things that I dread

Open your eyes, and open the doors
    Of a bright sun shining day

Glowing in your soul
    And burning to shine out

Many roads are dark and lonely
    These roads have attracted much traffic

Jesus is the light of a dark and lonely road
    He's a mother to the motherless

And a friend that sticketh
    Closer than any brother.

9 | AN INTRODUCTION TO SELF

I noticed one day
    Just who I was

Not just a body
    Passing through the world

Like a lonely ship out to sea
    Without a port, passes through

But rather a personality
    That piqued my interest

A character, cast in a role
    With many other supporting characters

Allowing that role to be
    Played out explicitly

Destined to take the academy awards
    Becoming the best of what I've become

Allowing my inner man to smile
    From the inside at what we consider humorous

Avoiding desperately not to fight
    With the inner man, it can only lead to confusion

BUILDING A VILLAGE

But rather flowing with the concerns
    Of life with respect to human dignity

Peeling through the layers of rotten fruit
    To find good fruit piercing through

A new found knowledge, levels
    Above my wildest expectations

An ocean of things that really do matter
    And not just a body passing through the scenes of the world

A partner which pushes me
    Beyond limitations and barriers

Wakes me when I'm sleep, but
    Gives me the peace to sleep when my eye lids are heavy

Feeling beautiful because something beautiful lives
    Inside me, making beautiful things happen everywhere I go

10 | A REACH BEYOUND MY GRIP

In my mind's eye,
I can see where I want to be.
The vision of a place
Which is separated by barriers unseen.

Like the view from
A prison window

It's barrier, a simple key to unlock
The steel gates which hold me bound

Or the rainbow just outside my window
Close enough to touch, yet separated

By height and distance and
A simple window pane.

11 | THE ROAD TO FREEDOM'S DOOR

All doors come with conditions

Open or closed

Locked or unlocked

Push or pull.

The invitation to pass through

Rely on your simple

Will and know how.

12 | ONCE WHITE, WHITE NO MORE

A shade of what originated
 As the purest form of white

Now have become varying shades
 Of cream, winter and off whites.

And a pure form of gray,
 White polluted with a drop of black.

Which really describes
 The soul of a man

In its purest forms
 Shall be whiter than snow.

But soon become
 Whites yellowing, dingy and spotted

When at a closer look was
 Really never quite white at all.

The stained, dusty and soiled
 In need of a lot of brighteners

Was really the varying forms of whites
 Which have surfaced in its place

Will the real pure white
 Please stand, and again I say stand.

13 | I CRIED, I PRAYED, I FOUGHT

In the heat of a
vicious moment
I cried.

In the consequences of
a lack of wisdom
I cried.

In the struggle of
day to day lack
I cried.

In the agony of
unanswered questions
I cried.

In the shame of an
uncovered truth
I cried.

In the face of a
losing battle
I cried.

PAMELA FIELDS

In the discomfort
of bondage
I cried.

In the midst of challenge
so great it hurts
I cried.

In the tangled
webs of a heap of mess
I cried.

In the valley of a
great mountain
I cried.

In the absence of
leadership and direction
I cried.

In the voyage of doom which drew
blood and tears
I cried.

In a place which required great courage
where I stood alone
I prayed.

In the hope
of winning
I fought.

Backed in the corner of a
bad situation
I won.

14 | BARRIERS

Barriers are not always
something you can see.
It's not always a physical
object, but there is another.

It is however, in the majority of the cases,
objects whether physical or otherwise...

Objects which will not let you pass,
and in these cases, the only way to pass
is to break through.

Breaking through barriers
that block finances.

Breaking through barriers
that stagnate my spiritual growth.

Breaking through barriers
mentally and physically so.

PAMELA FIELDS

Barriers which keep me in bondage
Reaching, never cease reaching.

Seeing with my focus, those
things I have desired.

Reaching and seeing
but these barriers

Got to break through
to the other side.

Too many have lost
sight of the focus

Have reverted to
have fallen from.

Regressed and have
Stepped back from

Too many have become complacent
to the "norms" of society.

Barriers won't go away
So I must break through!

15 | A GOOD STEWARD

Your lost represents
A lot of sorrow to all who knew her

Her memory is as fresh
As yesterday

Her life an action verb
Bringing many so much joy

With her great humor
And deeds of good-will

Never stop loving her
But know that her absence is heaven's gain

And that her soul was
Represented well in this realm

That you are extensions of
Who she was

A glimmer of her light
Is reflected in you:

PAMELA FIELDS

First her family
Secondly students who looked up to her

And thirdly the many who shared a friendship
With her, her peers' co-workers, acquaintance and colleagues

God has gained a good steward

In loving memory of Valerie Chappell

16 | LIFEGUARD

The lifeguard
Of my life

As I swim in
peaceful waters

The same lifeguard
when the storms are raging

And the waves
try to swallow me up whole

The same lifeguard
Which watches

My soul
day by day.

17 | BRINGING DELIVERANCE INTO FOCUS

Seeing what others see
     Concerning my situation

Feeling the claws of
     Pain with no outlet

Understanding that my focus
     Brings me to a different situation

A change regardless of
     The evidence of what others see

A focus which eases the pain
     Presenting an outlet which isn't

In the spirit of the mind's eye
     There is a reverse situation

There is an outlet which hides itself
     Above the things which are obvious in this life

Yes, there is a level which causes
     Men to forget the agony of his pain

A level where blessings are manifested
     And deliverance is sought through praise and worship

BUILDING A VILLAGE

A level in prayer and faith
    With the full power and anointing of God's Holy Word of Truth

When this level is reached then comes
    Manifestations of blessings and deliverance

But you have to see it, you have to focus to see it
    Bring deliverance into focus to be blessed.

18 | WINTER IS

Winter is the most serious of all seasons
    Autumn sounding a colorful warning as it passes through.

The shedding of its leaves revealing a very bare tree,
    As earth's little creatures store up food and nuts
        The birds have all flown south

Who and what ever ventures to stay
    Faces the silent chills of wintertime
        And humbles the spirit to prevail itself

The joy of the biggest holiday is celebrated
    The spirit of Christmas is whispered about
        And a coming New Year to look forward to

The spirit of winter humbles
    The spirit of Christmas passes
        And before the passing over into the New Year,

Another spirit shows up
    A serious spirit of death calls and brings
        The Angel of Death to snatch the souls
        Of many who will never wake up into the New Year.

19 | LEARNING TO FIGHT THE DEVIL

When the devil lodges camp
    working overtime to devise
        a plan to keep you down,

Aiming to conquer your
    mind and seeking to
        penetrate your heart,

Understand the Eve
    didn't have a chance
        against his subtle suggestions

So too will he make
    suggestions within your mind
        a battleground under constant attack

Keep guard of your mind
    against thoughts of indifference
        learn to fight the devil by first recognizing his tactics.

20 | GIVING AWAY A MIRACLE

I don't see the accomplishments
    Nor the rewards of labor

How many bricks do it take to
    Build one house?

The word of God saying
"The soul is the temple of the
Holy Ghost."

As I meet people on the street
And on the various places I go…

21 | HELP! LOVED ONE FOR RANSOM

HELP! Somebody's got your son.
   Somebody's got your daughter.
      Somebody's got your wife, your husband.

That somebody is the devil.
   Spiritual wickedness which can only be fought
      In the spirit with fasting and much prayer.

How is it that laughter is destroyed?
   How do you destroy goodness,
         Kindness,
            Gratitude
              Goodwill

Joy and peace toward another?
   How do you destroy love?
      How are these things destroyed?

In a word… the devil.
   A spiritual wickedness.

There is a way out.
   There's an answer.
      There is hope for your situation.

PAMELA FIELDS

**Learn how to fight for that somebody
In your family who has lost their hope, joy, peace
And even the freedom of their own minds; through
Addiction, and depression and spirits of suicide.**

Get your spiritual training at a Bible believing, Bible teaching church, one that exercise the Bible principals through precepts and examples.

22 | THE BEST TEACHER

One might say that experience is the best teacher.
    However, a good example
        Can teach just as much…

What are we teaching our children?
    What are we teaching our neighbor's children?
        Our nieces and nephews, what are we teaching them?

The list goes on and on.
    Someone may be learning
        Something from you right now.

Our words, sometimes fell to reach
    But our actions are more powerful than we think.
        It's on you, whether your examples are negative or positive.

23 | OUR OWN CHILDREN ARE AT STAKE

Our own children are at stake
    Against a world which advertise:

Greed, Lust, Sex
    Violence, and Negative Behavior.

There are other role models in this world
    You and Me…

Our children need to know that there are
    Rewards of joy, excitement, fun and other
        Learning experiences which can fulfill and last.

24 | GIFTS THAT LAST

Time out for gifs
    Which do not deal with the real problems
        Confronting today's generation of young people.

Gifts of good will and good deeds:
    Smiling
    Giving
    Goodness
    Kindness
    Gentleness
    Listening with the right ear
    Discerning when problems arise

These are gifts which will last a lifetime.
    But it's up to us to teach these gifts to them.
    It's up to us to show them during the course of life.

25 | ALL OF OUR CHILDREN ARE STARS

All of our children
    are stars.

There may be some you can reach
    better than I

And others I can reach better
    than you

But together, in perfect unity
    we must give positive messages

To supply the deficit which leads
    to the negative outcome in some of our youth today

Help me...

    I Beseech You | I Challenge You | I Invite You

BUILDING A VILLAGE
Construyendo un Pueblo
INTERMISSION

26 | THE FACE OF CRIME

The face of
    Crime, Sin and Shame

Is disguised beneath the
    Breath of temptation

And seduces unsuspecting
    Victims

That may yield because of a lack
    Of self-control and wisdom

Virtues of which today's youth
    Lack much.

27 | SOLUTIONS

Low Self-Esteem
    Unforgiveness
        Deep Seeded Hurt
            Drugs and Alcohol
                Lust, Sex and Tobacco
                    Violence and Rebellion

These are some of the problems
    Which face our youth today.

They need answers that help…
    A Band-Aid is a solution to a wound
        It is not, however, the answer to the problem.

Proper Direction
    People to Talk to
        People who are concerned
            Shown through deeds of Gentleness
            Kindness
                Sharing
                    Giving and
                        Goodness.

28 | OUR CHILDREN NEED

Our children need:

>Positive leadership not just
>Computers, T.V. and Radio

They need:

>Teachers who are not afraid of them
>
>Youth workers not leaders in name only.
>
>To utilize their minds according to the morale survival of mankind.
>
>Social discipline

But how, when they're not being taught? They can work every computer game, but never been introduced to proper conduct:

Gratitude	Goodness
Thankfulness	Temperance
Compassion	Faith
Humility	Gentleness
Meekness	Joy
Kindness	Love
And Peace	

PAMELA FIELDS

We are teachers in everything we do or say.
That's why T.V. have become less than an ally in this battle.
They need lessons in conduct which build positive character.

Our children need:

    Positive Leadership
    Positive Direction
    Positive Role Models
    To Develop A Positive Attitude

Too many of them are ending up wasted… We all need:

    A Positive Future

It can begin in our community… We can give our children a head start by giving this part of their learning a more serious attention!!!

29 | COME AS MY GUEST

COME:

LEARN	what you can about the Bible
OFFER	your leadership skills
BE	a role model to some of today's youth
PRAISE	God for His blessings to you
HEAR	the good news and how God lead His people from their bondage of sin
AS MY GUEST	to the Temple of The Most High Where the doors are opened in His Most Holy Name.

30 | NO OUTLET

A room filled with people
    Each experiencing his own pain.

What we do with the little room within our minds
    Seeking separate outlets.

Sorrowful, remorseful, fearful, and unexpected quivers
    Growing from the inside.

Little wonders, and a few doubts,
    Big maybes, but mostly I don't knows.

Unsure about what's to come
    Which causes this agonizing pain.

Not really knowing where to scratch
    Itch, itch, itch.

BUILDING A VILLAGE

The little room has a passage
    Which takes me far from here.

Awaken by the call of my name
    Day dreaming has a purpose.

But when I open my eyes again
    To answer the call

Reality places me right back
    Facing my pain with no outlet.

31 | WHOSE CHOICE

New challenges today I face
    As I stand for what I know.

Dodging choices of unrighteousness
    A challenge within myself.

Pills of bitterness keeps me
    In tune with the reality of injustice.

Caught between what I know
    And what I feel
    And what I smell to be a set up.

A trickster of great demeans
    Which polls on the mind.

Causing schemes of set ups
    Like cat and mice games.

Bugging you till you wear out
    Whose choice was this anyhow?

32 | A POCKET FULL OF JOY

The joy of the Lord is my
        strength…

Joy, one of the best ingredients of life,
        too many have tried life without.

When the cost of life's every experience
        adds up in pain…

When the simplest task ends
        up in struggle…

And around every corner lies
        the unexpected…

When you're living with ungratefulness
        and unforgiveness shows up at the door…

Take a pocket full of joy,
        and spread it everywhere you go.

33 | WITH ALL THE THINGS I KNOW TO DO

As I explore the many options
    at this point of destiny

Making a choice should seem easy
    with the many things I know to do.

Shall I:

    Work hard like a Hebrew slave
    Both night and day?

    Or stay in my chosen
    profession of skills?

    Shall I open a cookie bakery?

    Or take in lost children
    near and far?

    Or shall I become a great
    writer instead?

Piercing back the shambles of my life
    can seem quite a chore.

With all the things I know to do,
    it should be so easy to do.

BUILDING A VILLAGE

Easy once upon a time
      when life's aches and pain

Didn't rest so heavily at the wrist.

So Maybe I should become
      a teacher

A philosopher of education
      and a guide to knowledge.

34 | FAITH REMOVES THE CHALLENGE

In the face of weakness
    Faith removes the challenge.

Though I'm weak, am I made
    Strong through faith.

When the pressures of
    Life's ever so present

Like a tug-of-war
    Pulling across lines of scrimmage.

Touching to find the sore spots
    Of possible weakness.

Sore spots of tenderness
    Which makes me yield

Only when I'm clothed with the
    Strength of faith during these times
    Shall I be made strong.

Faith that takes me to the top of any mountain,
    Even on the dusty trail of any desert,
    Or in the midst of the open sea,
    In the storm or the thickest wilderness.

BUILDING A VILLAGE

Faith removes the doubt
    Which tugs at my mind.

Faith holds me up under
    The greatest of all pressures.

Faith evens the score which causes that
    Yield and works it all out for my good.

When I'm weak, then am I
    Made strong.

When I close my eyes,
    Faith removes the challenge.

35 | A SKETCH OF BEAUTY

With the pen, thoughts sketched
The frame of human character.

Then poured in it the
Likeness of God above.

Carefully drawing
Each detail.

Then smoothing out
The rough edges.

Filling in the clay
Whenever necessary.

Painting on the seeds
Of salvation.

36 | CUTTING ON THE LIGHT IN DARKNESS

Cutting on the light
in a dark, dark place.

Lights of understanding
priceless and rare

Feeling your way
when you simply need
to open your eyes.

37 | PORTRAIT OF A SERVANT

If words could paint my picture
    With details it would describe

Each day the brush would paint
    Its beauty in life to give.

Every last day of struggle,
    Struggle against its own wishes.

I know that this time,
    This time is not my own.

So much to give to those
    Who are in special need.

Even my last wish,
    I give, it's not my own.

Because this time that I have to give
    Is only but a short moment.

To make a difference,
    To complete an assignment
        To become the servant that I am.

BUILDING A VILLAGE

Lord, help my every selfish thought.
    Turn them into your kingdom's gain.

Inspire them to
    Create for you.

Direct them towards another
    Victory for you.

Take my life, it's yours
    I give it pure and free.

When you paint the portrait
    Of this servant,

Paint it with a smile and
    With every action verb.

Let it produce
    Joy, peace and progress

If words could paint
    My portrait

It wouldn't be just a picture
    But an action pack movie.

Deeds that pushes you over
    The threshold of confort.

PAMELA FIELDS

Tasks that try your
        Patience
                Self-control
                      And all the fruits of the spirit.

What you do for Christ
        Only will last.

Storing up heavenly treasures,
        Running the race of faith
                Keeping focus on the heavenly prize.

Running this race
        It's not given to the
                Swift nor to the strong.

But to the one who
        Endures.

Enduring being talked about
        Misunderstood,
                Lied on and forsaken.

Standing through the storms
        Of test and trails

Climbing levels of faith,
        To find greater levels

BUILDING A VILLAGE

Asking,
    Seeking,
        Knocking at the door of heaven for life's answers.

Swimming through floods
    Climbing mountains
        Running races
            And riding the storms of life.

If words could paint my portrait
    Paint it with a smile

And let it describe every
    Action word.

38 | MORE THAN YOU CAN IMAGINE

My eyes have cried
More tears than you can imagine,
Yet I live.

My tender heart have
Felt more pain
And yet I live.

My feelings have suffered
More hurt,
Yet I live.

The shadows of fear keeps
Lurking at me more than ever,
Yet I live.

Many dreams have ended
And faded in the midst of darkness
Yet I live.

My life have struggled
Through more mistakes,
And yet I live.

BUILDING A VILLAGE

I live,
       I live,
              I live.

When I fell, I got up
And lived.

When I lost yesterday,
I lived today, and today, I won.

Every day, I win
A new opportunity to live.

And because I cried more than
You can imagine yesterday,

Today I live, a brand new
Opportunity, and today I cry no more.

39 | THIS OLD WORLD HAVE A HEAVEN

Beyond the firmaments
    And above the clouds
        The stars, the moon and the sun,
Lies heaven.

Beyond the greatest wonders
    In the gaps of the basic element of time,
        Confusion, addiction and the agony of pain.
Lies heaven.

In the balance of untimely pitfalls
    An angle from where I stand,
        I can't control,
But there is a heaven.

In a world just beyond the sight,
    An eternal home awaits,
        Because the Father willed it to be so,
There is a heaven.

BUILDING A VILLAGE

But first I must earn
    My heavenly crown,
        A position and a right to claim
Cause there is a heaven.

Laying aside every weight
    Letting nothing separate me from God's love,
        Seeking first the kingdom,
There is a heaven.

Out of all the things of the world
    I can't think of any one thing
        Which is greater,
There is a heaven.

A beauty that awaits
    This sluggish son of man
        Flesh and bones which can only return back to dust,
There is a heaven.

40 | A GARDEN OF FLOWERS

IN THE PROCESS OF LIFE
Great and precious

THERE AWAKENS WITHIN
Bullets of myself

SHOOTING TOWARDS THE THINGS
That identify my rightful character

IN THE EVOLUTION OF TIME
Peace will come
Joy will come.

IN AND OUT AND BETWEEN
Bitter pills

THERE IS A GARDEN OF FLOWERS
Just outside of my grief.

41 | OLE MY RAGGEDY SOUL

I feel so raggedy
    Like a raggedy Ann doll
        Only with feelings, attitude and a lot of character.

Like a Boxer
    Just hanging in there, as the bell sounds
        And I stagger over to the time out corner.

Manager squirts water in my mouth
    Slaps me on the cheeks a couple of times
        And gives me his best pep talk.

The only reasons I won't just fall out and faint
    Is because someone told me the victory is mine
        And because the other player is raggedy too.

Sometimes you have to just stay in the fight
    For the race is not given to the swift, nor to the strong
        But to the one which endure until the end.

All I got to do is stand,
    Ole my raggedy soul.

42 | A SHADOW IN THE HEART

You're the space of a kingdom,
    You're the image of a sky.

Come see about me,
    My Fair Prince.

I am shaking, trembling and I am weak.

In the clutter of my sin,
    Come see about me!

My true love has become my weakness.
The candy that I love, has rotted my teeth.
The fatback causes my blood pressure to rise.
Making more money than I should because of the lie.
Smoking on the cigarette that is choking me,
    And causes me cancer.
Popping my fingers to the music on the radio,
    Oh, oh, oh.
My true love has become my weakness.

In the clutter of my sin,
    Come see about me!

BUILDING A VILLAGE

For I am shaking and trembling, I am weak.

I repent, for the joy of the Lord is my strength.

In the abundance of gladness
     My weakness is but a shadow
     Which visited me in the weakest hour, I confess.

In the heat of a sunny day,
     The soul of a man seeks
     The shadow of a shady tree.

So, it is in the abundance of joy
     Does the soul entertain
     The desires of the shadow thoughts of his heart

The shadow thoughts,
     Which lie in wait
     Then pounces upon the opportunity of desire
     In the weakest hour.

Come see about me,
     My Fair Prince!

I am shaking and trembling and weak.

In the clutter of my sin,
     Come see about me!

Erase the transgression,
     Blot out the stain.

Then create in me a clean heart,
     And renew a right spirit in me.

PAMELA FIELDS

Wash me in the blood,
    Till I sin no more.

O' wretched man that I am,
    In thee I shall put no trust.

Thank you, Paul,
For your instructions are clear.

Thank you, David,
For showing me how to have a repentful heart

Thank you, Solomon,
For giving me to understand the dangers of abundance.

Thank you, Job,
For giving me to know that abundance is not the sin,
And for helping me to understand the rewards of faith
Even in the depth of trails.

Thank you, Abraham, Isaac and Jacob,
Who called upon the Lord in the wilderness of shadows.

Thank you, Moses,
For God used you mightily even though
Your sins were great, you obeyed the instructions of
the Lord.

Thank you, Jesus,
Who carried the sins of the whole world upon shoulders
of flesh.

    And became the only sacrifice that the world
    would ever need
    Through this, restored men back to God.

BUILDING A VILLAGE

All these men had a purpose to fulfill
    For this I am eternally grateful.
    Because in my flesh dwells no good thing.

My forefathers and brethrens
    Teaches me the grace and mercy of God the Father.
    And the righteousness of Jesus Christ our Lord and Saviour.

Now I have peace in the valley,
    I can conquer the mountain.

There ain't no shady trees sprouting up in my heart
    And no seed sprouting shady trees.

My flesh died,
    When I pulled up the root of that old shady tree.

Sin hides in darkness
    In the comfort of that old shady tree, lurks the shadow of sin.

In the abundance of joy,
    The sun shineth in my heart.

At the dawn of a new day,
    New mercies I give unto you,
    Amen.

43 | FREEDOM
MEAN CHOICES

We are all children like unto the prodigal son, everyone.
When our Father is rich in spirit, in health and in wealth.
Rich, I tell you, every one of us.

Do you not know that some of us never come to ourselves?
Some of us parish in the uncertain estate of poverty, and lack.
Confused by our apparent circumstances of weakness,
      Brought on by sickness and diseases.

Yes, we whom have confessed our Saviour to be the Lord Jesus Christ
We have allowed His dying to be in vain when our living is in shame.
      Get it together Child.

Listen to the proverbs of wisdom, and let the psalmist instruct you.
      Stand up and command the spirits of destiny.
      Your adoption papers are recorded on high.

      Your Father is rich, full of majesty and power.
            Royal in all His might.
      Clothe yourself in the garment of your heritage.

      Let your very posture, your ora prove you.
            Stand tall and take your place.

BUILDING A VILLAGE

Say to the angels of your Father's to attend to your needs.
Command the angels of destruction that you have parted company with them. So part fellowship with the angels of lack, sickness and poverty. And surround yourself in the company of ministering angels full of might and power to move in our behalf and to open doors no man can close.

    Breathe the breath of freedom forever and ever.

    Come to the hours of your Father's and let your confession
    Command your physical rights to the Kingdom right here on
    Earth.

        And commune with your Father,
        Sup with Him, and He'll sup with you.

    He'll give you the best of calves and clothe you in royalty.
    You know the story, as it's told in Luke 15:11-31.
    It's written in the book of Luke for this reason,
    So that you'll know you have a kingdom awaiting.

44 | THE PRAYER OF A SERVANT

How can I not know the right thing to do?
When you've placed so many at my hands.

I need more funds you see
To sufficiently run this place.

My children are in rags
When they are your children too.

When I took this task
I believed that you'd help me.

Look at this dusty place
The cupboard is scarce
Still, what must I do?

The King's attention
He's sitting on all that wealth.

Please, Dear God, I pray
The King's attention, there must be a way.

45 | THE VOICE OF GOD

Yes, I've placed so many at your hand
    Because you know the right thing to do
        And because I trusted you with these souls.

The answer is within
    For I placed special gifts within
    Each child, you'll see.

Your help is near
    From the inside you see.

What you must do is prepare
    An acceptable gift

The King's attention
    You already have

For I am the King of kings
    You have my attention
        The way is from within.

46 | SHALLOW WAVES

A knee-high storm
At the sea shore of life.

47 | LIVING THROUGH THE STORM

At the crack of thunder's
Bellow

Lightening's flash though unheard

At the peak of a serious storm,
Thunder and lightning had
Center stage.

One would think that they worked
Together.

Hand in hand to compliment each other
And because you rarely saw one without
The other

But at the peak of this storm
Inside the storm of life peeped

Only to discover that it was one
Against the other

Thunder's crack, Lightening's flash.

PAMELA FIELDS

All of a sudden, the sun began to
Shine and the curtains dropped
On that storm.

The sun seemed to say
Behave yourself

And the storm had to obey
It had to cease.

The thunder simmered down
And the lightening did too.

In the middle of the storm,
The sun seemed to say, peace be still.

I'm reminded of another storm
Where the Son merely spoke the words
"Peace be still," and the storm ceased.

48 | NEXT

Your next is right over the hill
And although that hill might
Seem like a mountain,

Some people's next can't
Even be heard, and so
They continue in the wrong
Direction and miss their turn.

Think about that when you know
       You've done your best
       When you've passed the test
       Weary and in need of rest

Don't you dare stop,
       If you finish last, finish the race
       When you've done all to stand, stand therefore
       If trouble seem in the way, pray with faith

Get up!
Dry your eyes,
You got this!
NEXT!

49 | A COLOR SPLASH

Maybe it's because I work with

Black and white

Black and white people

Black and white print

Black and white situations

So much black and white

A little color

Splashed in the middle

Of the day

Would be very much appreciated.

50 | FIRST LIGHT A.D.

Once upon a campfire
Light

As we sat telling stories
In the night

As we toasted marshmallows
Like fires of light on our sticks

And strange noises could be
Heard in the thick of the night

Then the time came when
We all retired into our tents

And behold, a voice spoke to me
Saying, "come," and again
The voice said "come."

Then I said "I'm afraid wait until
I light my candlestick."

Then the voice of the Lord
Spoke, "come, I am the light."

PAMELA FIELDS

ACKNOWLEDGMENTS

First and foremost, I'd like to thank God for allowing me to go through my journey of life in which I have been able to learn and grow from my circumstances, and change my challenges into this beautiful work of art and book series of poems.

And to my mother, Leola Reynolds, whom told the best stories when I was growing up. My love for her and her stories as she told us as we were growing up were quite splendid.

And to my readers, I am grateful for your support I'd like to offer some wisdom. When an older person has a story to tell, sit down and listen because it will be a good story, one of true wisdom.

ABOUT THE AUTHOR

Born to Gentle Frank Fields and Leola Reynolds, Pamela Fields grew up on the south side of Chicago, Illinois, where she attended several elementary schools and Wendell Phillips High School, all schools located in Chicago, Illinois. She also attended Harold Washington Junior College and would go on to major is Early Childhood Education. She later attended Prestige Nurse Aide Training Academy, where she attained her certification as a CNA. Both of the selected majors were encouraged by her experiences of not wanting any child to be left behind, nor any older adult left uncared for.

Fields held the position of being the oldest of her siblings, one sister, and two brothers. She refers to her brothers and sister as stair-steps as each sibling is one year apart from the other. Fields acknowledge her siblings and Richard Reynolds, her superhero and second husband to her mother, for preparing her to understand and learn several tactics of dealing with the way of the world. Fields has three children: Nikia Fields, Edward Fields, and Shana Edwards, and she loves them all dearly. Her children have blessed her with eight grandchildren, and Fields continues to shower them with the educational packages from her homemade learning lessons.

PAMELA FIELDS

Getting into the professional side of life, Fields was employed at several early learning centers. She also worked as a CNA on weekends, and she spent a few evening hours taking care of her mother. Her years of employment with others have led her to her Happily Ever After, becoming a future best-selling author with S.H.E. PUBLISHING LLC, and starting up two businesses simultaneously, one being K.I.N.D.N.E.S.S. Kare (*Keys IN Developing & Navigating Effective Social Solutions*), a childcare service, and Pam's Baking Handz.

Ultimately, Fields purpose and passion is to bring together ordinary people like you and me with the commitment to encourage us to love one another. She believes that it's the small efforts of a friendly smile, the gift of gratitude, praying for one another, and small acts of kindness that will change the world one day, one hour, and one second at a time. It only takes a second to yield a smile and patience doesn't cost anything.

Thanks for reading!
Please add a short review on
Amazon and S.H.E. PUBLISHING LLC.
Let me know your thoughts!

www.ingramcontent.com/pod-product-compliance
Lightning Source LLC
LaVergne TN
LVHW032006070526
838202LV00058B/6319